Jokes for Kids!

101 Jokes for Little Kids - Big & Small!

By IP Grinning

Jokes for Kids!

Joke Books for Kids

Copyright © 2014 IP Grinning

ISBN: 9781500713331

What did the daddy bee say to the naughty bee?
Bee-hive yourself!

What do you call polar cows?
Eski-moos!

Why don't donkeys make good dancers?
Because they've got two left feet!

Why don't crabs share their food?
Because they're shellfish!

What did the policeman do when he caught the elephant that ran away with the circus?
Told her to take it back!

Why does a tiger have stripes?
So it won't be spotted!

What did the rats play at recess?
Hide and squeak!

◆

What did the seaweed shout when a fish began to eat it?
Kelp! Kelp!

◆

Why don't elephants ride motorbikes?
They can't fit their trunks in the helmets!

◆

Why do dogs get so hot at the beach?
They wear a coat and pants!

What goes "knock knock woof?"
A labra-door!

Why would an octopus vs. squid war be terrible?
Because they are so well-armed!

♦

Why wouldn't they let the butterfly into the dance?
It was a moth ball!

♦

What do you call skeletons that stay in bed all day?
Lazy bones!

♦

What do you call a male cow taking an afternoon nap?
A bulldozer!

What do you call a flying elephant?
An ele-copter!

Why does no-one ever hear pterodactyls using the bathroom?
Because they have a silent P!

◆

Why does the ocean not allow underwater playgrounds?
It's afraid of sea-saws!

◆

Why do you rarely see a lionfish?
They can't hold the rods with their paws!

◆

What do you call a bee born in May?
A maybe!

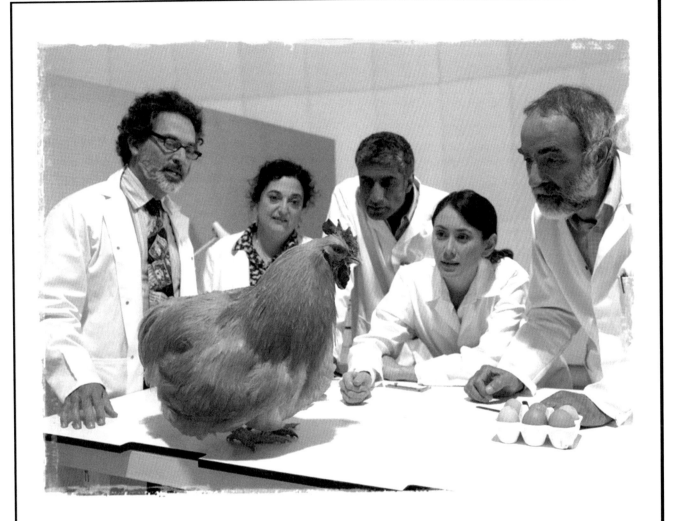

Doctor, doctor, I can't stop clucking and I'm scared!
Oh don't be such a chicken!

What do you call a man floating in the sea?

Bob!

Why was the glow worm unhappy?

She realized she wasn't that bright!

What happened to the man who crossed a leaky faucet with a dinosaur?

He got a drip-lodocus!

Why was the baby ant confused?

Because all his uncles were ants!

When do ghosts appear?
Just before someone screams!

Why was the cemetery crowded?
Everyone was dying to get in!

◆

Doctor, doctor, I keep thinking I'm a snowman!
Keep cool and I'll be with you in a moment!

◆

Why should you never go to a theater on the moon?
It lacks atmosphere!

◆

Why was Baron Frankenstein good around strangers?
He could make friends easily!

What happened to the vampire who entered the race?
He finished neck and neck!

History teacher: Why does history repeat itself?

Pupil: Because no-one listens in history lessons!

◆

What happened to the man who crossed a Lego set with a snake?

He got a boa constructor!

◆

Why was the alien green?

It hadn't taken its space sickness pills!

◆

Why don't chickens like humans?

We beat eggs!

What's green and eats chocolate ice cream?
A choco-dile!

What happened to the man who crossed a cat with a lemon?
He ended up with a sourpuss!

◆

Why do witches have to be careful never to get angry on a broomstick?
In case they fly off the handle!

◆

What kind of dinosaur was always hurting itself?
Really-saurus!

◆

Why do fish stay away from restaurants?
They are scared of getting battered!

What did the snail say on the turtle's back?
Weeeeeeee!

Why do jockeys ride horses?
Because they are too heavy to carry!

◆

Why do koalas never wear socks?
They prefer bear feet!

◆

What happened to the man who crossed a cat with knee-length shoes?
He got puss in boots!

◆

Why do librarians often talk about silent vegetables?
Because they are always saying "Quiet peas"!

Doctor, doctor! I need glasses!
You certainly do, madam. This is a cake shop!

Why do male deer always need braces?
They have buck teeth!

◆

History teacher: Where was the Declaration of Independence signed?
Pupil: At the bottom!

Why do museums have old dinosaur bones?
They can't afford new ones!

◆

Why do cows like to do on a night out?
Go to watch moo-sicals!

What did the cyclops teacher say to the class?
I've got my eye on you!

Teacher: Where might you find the English Channel?

Pupil: I don't know, is it near the MTV channel?

◆

Why do aliens wear helmets?

So they don't scare themselves when they look in the mirror!

Why did the vampire go to the doctor?

Because of the coffing!

◆

What kind of dinosaur was always crashing trucks?

Tyrannosaurus wrecks!

What do you call a penguin in the desert?
Lost!

Why do cows think they should group together in fields?
It's just what they herd!

Why do dogs always run in circles?
Because they don't know how many sides a rectangle has!

Why do dogs bury bones in the back yard?
Because they are not allowed to bury them in the kitchen!

Why didn't the two worms go on Noah's Ark in an apple?
Because they all had to go on in pairs!

Mum: Chris, have you taken a bath?
Boy: No, have you lost one?

Why do elephants sit still on marshmallows?
They don't want to fall in the hot chocolate!

◆

Why did the witch travel on a broom?
She had nowhere to plug in the vacuum cleaner!

◆

Why did the wood worm spend most of its time alone?
Because it was always boring!

◆

Why did the one-handed man cross the road?
To get to the second hand shop!

Who delivers Christmas presents to jungle animals?
Santa claws!

Why did the otter cross the road?

To get to the otter side!

◆

Why did the owl say, "Quack, quack, tweet, tweet"?

It didn't give a hoot!

◆

Why do elephants avoid the beach?

They can't keep their trunks up!

◆

Why did the teacher describe the boy's test results as underwater?

Because they were below 'C' level!

**Why didn't the skeleton go to the dance?
He had no body to go with!**

Doctor, doctor, I've been kicked out of the baseball team - I keep dropping the ball!

Don't worry - what you have is not catching!

◆

Why did the crazy space alien eat a couch and three chairs?

It had a suite tooth!

◆

Teacher: Where are the Great Plains?

Pupil: In the airport!

◆

Why did the dinosaur never forget to lock its front door?

Because tyrannosaurus checks!

How did the astronaut avoid getting burned when he visited the Sun?
He went at night!

Why did the crab cross the beach?
To get to the other tide!

◆

Why did the elephant paint its toenails red?
To hide in the cherry tree!

◆

Teacher: When was the last time your eyes were checked?
Boy: Never... they've always been brown!

◆

What happened when a man tried to cross a tiger with a sheep?
He had to get a new sheep!

Doctor, doctor, how long can you live without a brain?
I'm not sure, how old are you?

Doctor, doctor, I can't get to sleep!

Lay on the edge of the bed and you'll soon drop off!

◆

What happened when an elephant sat in front of a policeman at the movies?

He missed most of the film!

◆

What happened when Baron Frankenstein saw a bare-necked corpse walking around?

He made a bolt for it!

What do you call a mosquito in a metal suit?
A bite in shining armor!

What happened to the man who crossed a cockerel, a poodle and a ghost?
He got a cocker poodle boo!

THE END

Thank you for buying our book - do you want another?

To show our appreciation we are offering you a completely free book!
Visit the link below to claim your FREE pdf book.

ipfactly.com/free-joke-book

Thank you for reading!

Thank you so much for buying this book. I hope you've enjoyed reading it as much as I enjoyed writing it.

For more joke books search for: IP Grinning at Amazon.com

69672934R00024

Made in the USA
Lexington, KY
03 November 2017